The Rules of the AI Road

Archistry Press
First Edition
March 2025

Softcover ISBN: 979-8-9925425-3-0
e-book ISBN: 979-8-9925425-4-7

OutsideTheCollective.AI

OutsideTheCollective.AI

Contents

OutsideTheCollective.AI

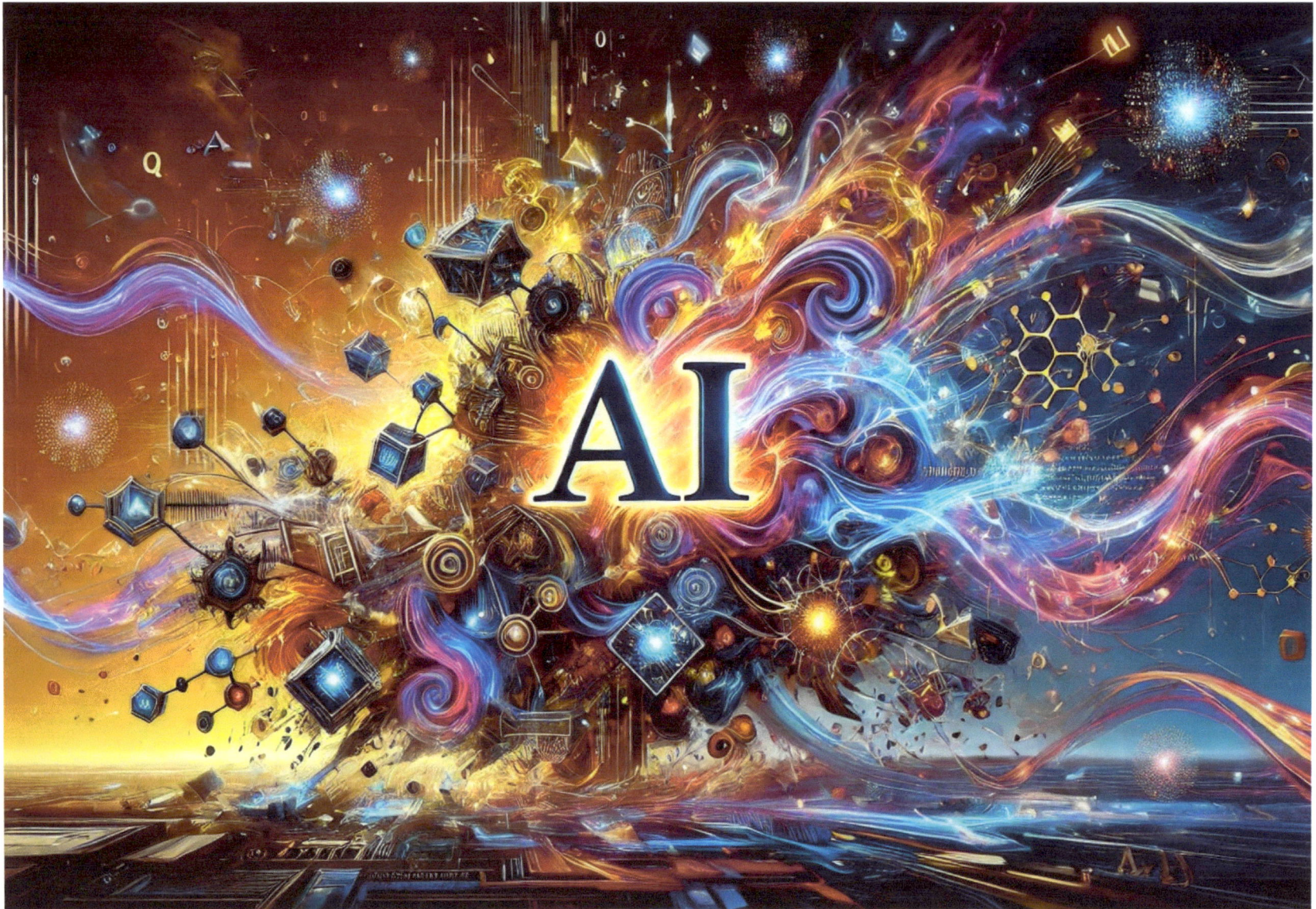

Understanding the Rise of AI

There's no question that we are living in the "Age of AI." In the last two years, there's been an explosion of hype about "artificial intelligence" or AI, and it's quickly become an essential part of daily work for millions of people. It's no longer just the technology toy or niche novelty it once was. Now, it's everywhere, and more of our work — and more of our lives — will become dependent on AI. How much you understand the implications of the technology of AI and **the way you use it will ultimately decide whether AI will make you unstoppable or irrelevant**.

If you want to get the most out of the potential power of AI without falling into its common pitfalls and traps, you need to understand what AI is and how it works. Because if you don't, then you'll be asking AI tools to do

things for you they're not really designed to do, and, without you realizing it, AI could give you the wrong information, tell you things that aren't actually true, and lead you to create things that would ultimately undermine your credibility, or maybe even get you fired.

Today's AI tools can easily blur the line between content you create and what's created by the tools. In fact, it can eliminate that line altogether, because more and more people are relying on AI to create everything from social media posts to blogs to emails to reports to even binding legal contracts. But the worst part of this is that **people are surrendering their creativity, judgment and professional value** to the complex calculations of what's really just a fancy computer program. When this happens, it's easy for you to think that if there's a mistake, you can blame it on the AI tools. You can't. The tools can't think, and they can't be accountable for anything. The only one who can be accountable for anything created by AI is the person who asked AI for it to be created.

AI is a branch of computer science that's been around for decades. Its goal is to demonstrate the possibility of creating "artificial intelligence" that allows computers to perform things typically done by humans because they have the ability to think, classify information and objects, make judgments and have opinions about information, issues and situations. However, AI is nothing more than a computer program, much like Microsoft Word or Excel. The difference is in the way you interact with it and the way it responds to you

By design, AI tools provide a way for you to "talk" to them just like you would a real person. In fact, it's becoming more and more common to really talk to AI tools rather than having to type. But whether you're typing or talking to AI, the interactions you have, and the responses you get, can sound deceptively "normal," conversational...and even human.

However, the reality is much different. Under the covers, those human-sounding responses are just the result of millions of sophisticated calculations. It's really just math, because based on what you tell an AI tool or ask it, it compares the words you use to words it already knows about and has analyzed. Based on those calculations, it assembles words by number, much like the paint-by-number pictures you might have done as a kid. Those numbers tell it which words are most likely to appear next to each other, and based on the computation it does, it generates a response for you.

There is nothing more "intelligent" about AI than that. It has no real knowledge or understanding of the words you say, and it doesn't have any real knowledge or understanding of the words it "says" to you. However, since the calculations it uses are

OutsideTheCollective.AI

created based on analyzing millions and millions of different documents, articles, blog posts and even video, it can quite successfully "sound" human in its responses. It can even sound confident, helpful or like it's being funny or joking around with you about something.

But it isn't real.

And that sense of "humanity" you may feel isn't real because it is just the response from a fancy computer program. It's a program that's analyzing your words and comparing them to the words it knows so that it can try its best to give you an answer you want. But there's the problem— that answer is actually one of many.

The way we interact with AI triggers our natural instincts to unconsciously trust the responses we get. AI responds so "naturally" and seems so "human" in the way you can talk to it that we're inclined to just believe it's intelligent. Its responses seem real,

true and useful. But AI can't actually evaluate those traits at all. **You are the only one who can really know whether you get useful, helpful and valid responses from an AI system.**

At first this might seem a little scary, because you might now have some concerns about using AI in your own life and work. Having these concerns is fine, perfectly normal and, in fact, necessary if you want to be able to fully embrace the power of today's AI tools and set yourself up for being ahead of everyone else. If you do this, you'll be ahead of people who are lulled into the trap of thinking that AI actually understands anything, or that it's really nothing more than just a fancy, content-generating calculator with a big vocabulary. This knowledge gives you power, because it helps **keep you in control** and helps make sure you **get the most out of your interactions with AI**.

While you might not realize it now, the degree to which **you remain in control**

of your use of AI is important. I mentioned earlier that AI is using calculations to determine which words it reflects back to you in its responses. That means it's learning from you with every response it gives, but it's also training you too. When you don't get the answers you like, or which make sense, you start to change the way you're interacting with it, hoping for a better outcome or response. You change the way you ask for things, or, after several minutes – or even hours – of frustration, you might just accept one of its responses as "good enough" and move on with your next task.

It's very easy to find yourself much further from your original goals and intentions at the end of an interaction with AI than you may realize. The more you fail to recognize this drift, and the more you take what AI provides automatically, and without really thinking about what is happening, the more likely you are to end up sounding just like everyone else. Worse yet, you might quickly reach the point where "just ask AI" is the default reflex for even the most basic task you would ordinarily have done yourself. A task which you believe is now much easier and faster to do with the help of AI.

Falling into these traps is how you become part of "The Collective™," where everyone looks the same, sounds the same, uses the same kinds of images, repeats and amplifies the same information, and basically becomes so dependent on AI to do things that they don't even feel confident to write a two-line email without "checking it" using AI.

In this brief guide, *The Rules of the AI Road™*, I'm going to introduce you to some lessons I've learned from using today's advanced AI tools on a daily basis. I actually love what today's AI tools can help me do, and I want you to feel the same. However, one of the main reasons that I'm more productive than most people is that I stay in control of what I'm doing, and

I'm aware of when AI might be "going off the rails" just a bit. I can only do this because I understand how the underlying technology works.

By understanding how the technology works, and how easy it is to fall into the most common traps that will unwillingly and subtly suck you into The Collective, **you too will have the power to stay in the driver's seat when you're using AI instead of letting AI drive you**.

My background is in computer science, and I've written software professionally, designed massive solutions for government and industry and I've been on the cutting edge of some of the alternative approaches and technologies in the AI space for more than 20 years.

I'm sharing this information with you so that you too can understand some of what I've learned about AI in a way that helps you get the most out of these tools today, **making you faster,**

more productive and ultimately accelerating your own growth and development, both personally and professionally. The reality is that you can only accomplish these things if you truly understand the nature of the tools you're using. If you don't, you're going to end up using hammers to crack eggs or you're going to try to paint your house with your toothbrush. In either case, it's the wrong tool for the job or you're using the tool the wrong way.

Since modern AI is intentionally designed to look, "feel" and sound like humans, we need to be even more acutely aware that it isn't—otherwise, we can fall into several traps that will lead us down a path of dependency, ignorance and blind trust in the output and responses we get from AI. Any one of these leads to a potential helplessness that could ultimately end up reducing our ability to think critically, understand the world, and be able to excel in our professional careers and our personal lives.

With this guide, I've distilled some fundamental "rules of the road" I've discovered as part of my own growing use and expertise in getting the most out of AI. I want to share it with you so that you can fully embrace what it's capable of doing to **help you stand out and stay ahead of the pack**—but without falling into the traps and pitfalls that I see many people do.

This guide isn't another set of "awesome prompts" or a basic introduction on "how to use AI." If you want to thrive in the Age of AI, you need much more. Most people using AI today are relying on only basic tips and training – either for free or from expensive AI literacy and certification programs – that just tells you how to do specific tasks or how to use AI "responsibly" within your job so that you don't inadvertently share sensitive information with the rest of the world.

This basic information is necessary to get you started and keep you and your organization safe professionally and compliant with privacy laws. However, if you stopped there, and you only use AI tools to automate or perform specific tasks, this is barely scratching the surface of what you can potentially accomplish with AI.

Once you clearly understand what AI is, and where the dangers in using it lie, you can use it to its full potential. You don't have to fear it. You don't have to worry about whether it's steering you the wrong way. Instead, if you have the right understanding and a solid framework you know will keep you safe, **you can boldly step into using AI effectively**—without worrying about losing control, or, worse yet, without losing that aspect of you that makes your contributions to your work and the world truly unique. This guide gives you exactly such a framework.

Inside this guide, I've pulled together a set of 5 underlying **principles** that define the "rules of engagement" for AI, 3 critical "AI **reflexes**" that give you practical, reliable sanity checks to use during every interaction with AI and the 5 "**rules** of the road" that will help you get the most out of AI by seamlessly integrating it into your work without becoming dependent on it—**making AI an accelerant for your productivity**.

These are the principles, reflexes and rules I use every day in my own interactions, and they've helped me achieve "next level" results with AI. I hope they do the same for you so you too can **stay outside The Collective**.

Andrew S. Townley

—

Andrew S. Townley
Archistry Chief Executive

OutsideTheCollective.AI

5 Unbreakable Principles of AI

A **principle** is a statement of basic law or truth about something that should never change. If a statement changes, then that statement can't be a principle, by definition. Based on a fundamental understanding of the way the technologies currently used in mainstream AI work, I've come up with 5 unbreakable truths about AI. These truths, if forgotten, can result in you slipping slowly into The Collective where everyone thinks the same thoughts, says the same things and even shares the same core beliefs.

Each of these principles will first be defined and then explained. I'll give you the core truth behind each principle, what it really means and why it matters to you as you engage and use AI in your daily life.

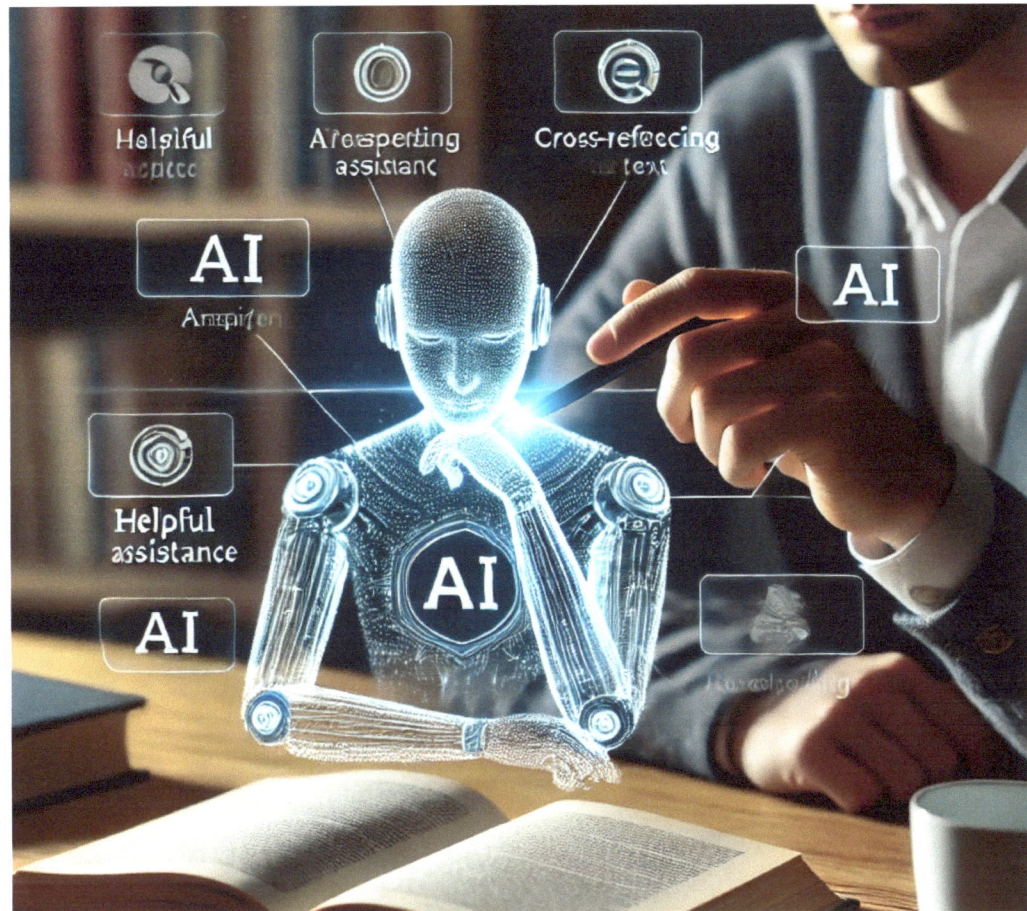

OutsideTheCollective.AI

AI isn't just changing how we work; it's changing how we think. Most people don't realize the degree to which AI is a "mental filter." When you use AI, it frames what's possible, shapes decisions and influences how we process information. **If you're not actively managing your AI interactions, you're being shaped by them instead**.

Once you integrate these principles into the way you think about the work you do with AI, you'll be able to easily get the most out of AI, and you'll be able to make sure you're the one driving AI instead of the other way around. When you can do that, then you'll certainly **stay outside The Collective and safely in control**.

Here is the list of the 5 principles covered in this section:

Principle 1: AI is not intelligent because AI is just a computer. It has no understanding, and therefore, it

can't exercise the judgment required to make any kind of decision.

Principle 2: AI is biased because an AI tool bases its responses on only the information used to build them. If the foundation of its responses is biased, what it generates for you will be too.

Principle 3: AI is influencing you because it is designed to seem "right" and like it knows exactly what you should do next. The more you interact with AI, the more likely you are to naturally accept its responses and suggestions at face value.

Principle 4: AI doesn't replace your brain because AI doesn't know anything and it has no capability for judgment; it can't think. Only you can think, and you can't let AI do it for you.

Principle 5: AI is a mirror because it can only tell you things that have been said or done before, based on the information used to build it. However, since it only does what you tell it to do,

it's also a mirror of your thinking and where you may have blind spots.

Principle 1: AI is not Intelligent

The Truth

AI is just an application. It looks more complicated than it is because you can interact with it using normal words, sentences and even by using your voice. However sophisticated and knowledgeable it might seem, AI is still not intelligent.

The "intelligence" of AI just means it responds with something that looks like intelligence on the surface. AI is created to make us <u>believe</u> it is intelligent – that it thinks – but in reality, this is impossible. AI works by effectively using a big dictionary of information, where that dictionary is just a list of normal words associated with a number. The math the AI tool uses is probability, and that means that it has analyzed millions and millions of sentences and "learned" from these sentences which words appear together more when talking about a given topic. However, because it's just a calculation, and it doesn't truly understand what any of those words mean, it's really just guessing. It's using a mathematical "crystal ball" to tell you things that sound right based on what you asked.

That's right. Today's AI's "intelligence" is an illusion – a fancy magic trick – performed millions of times a second every time you ask it for something.

What It Means

The implications of AI's lack of intelligence are that while there's a good chance it might be able to generate something useful, it might not. What you get all depends on what information was used to build that dictionary or table mapping the numbers with the words and their relationships to each other. If what you want to know was talked about correctly in many of the different

documents used to build the AI you're using, often called "training data," then you have a higher chance of getting something that is correct. However, if you're asking about something that was either not covered in the training data or which was more commonly stated incorrectly than correctly, then your chances of getting the wrong answer are much higher.

Since **AI can't think**, that means **it can't understand**. And if it can't understand, then **it has no beliefs**—about anything: especially right or wrong. And because it has no beliefs, **there's no way it can truly have any kind of judgment about the correctness, quality or suitability of anything it says or creates** for what you ultimately are trying to do.

Why It Matters

You can now have a conversation with AI for hours, just by talking to it and listening to what it says back to you. You're talking to it normally, and the voice you hear doesn't sound like a

robot from an old movie or TV show. It sounds like a person.

When you're typing or talking to an AI system, you're using natural language. You're using complex sentences. You're typing to AI the same way you'd type a text message to your friends or colleagues—or even the same way you'd write an article or blog post. When you talk to it, it's just like someone's on a speakerphone.

Because of the advances in the technologies that wrap that simple, number-crunching core of AI, it's getting harder and harder to tell what's been created by a human and what's been created by AI. It's not an accident. It's been done deliberately.

The AI tool designers are trying to make it easier for you to use and to explain to AI what you want, and they're trying to make it easier for you to understand, apply and use whatever comes out of it. As the technology advances, it becomes closer and closer to being the same "feel" and experience you would have talking to someone else or reading an email from your boss.

The ultimate irony is that the more successful technologists are in making AI respond and sound like people, the less likely we are to remember that we're dealing with a machine. A machine that doesn't understand what it's saying. A machine that doesn't know what's right and wrong, and a machine that may very well be giving us the equivalent of a sugary snack: something that looks good and tastes good initially, but which might end up not being good for us or what we really need at the time.

That doesn't mean AI is bad. Far from it. Today's AI is allowing people to do things they've never been able to do before and in a much shorter time. But you can't ever forget that it's still a machine. And if it's a machine, **not only can it make mistakes. It won't even realize it's made them. You are the only one who can do that.**

Principle 2: AI Is Biased

The Truth

Biases have become quite a big deal over the last few years, and there's a good reason: our biases affect the way we see the world and how we respond in certain situations. However, sometimes people get the idea that biases are inherently bad. They're not. In fact, our ability to function in society wouldn't be possible without our biases, because otherwise we'd have to stop and deliberately think about everything we did—even the small stuff. While AI can't think, that doesn't mean it can't be biased.

However, when we talk about AI being biased, it's not quite the same thing as it is for a human. Bias in AI tools is only about what they "know" from the information they've been given. Bias in humans is a combination of what they know and what they believe about the world. Bias in AI determines what appears in the responses it generates.

Any response from AI can only draw from information it is given. If you give it correct, balanced and useful information, then there's a good chance that's what you're going to get back when you ask it a question. However, unlike humans who can become aware of their biases and decide to act differently, **the biases of AI are "baked in" from the selection of the information it's given—either from the beginning or as it evolves**.

What It Means

If the information an AI tool was given is incorrect, incomplete or deliberately crafted to lead someone to a certain understanding or belief about something, then the response you get from AI will also have the same inaccuracies, missing pieces and potentially influential or even subversive overtones. Because AI can't understand what it's saying, and it can't judge better from worse, right from wrong or love from hate, it's simply an assembler and amplifier of whatever is inside it.

Asking AI about the topic in different ways or trying to get it to give a different opinion, answer or to "fill in the gaps" can be a futile exercise. AI tools can't tell you things they don't have, so, **without adding more information and calculating new entries in its dictionary, AI will give you the same misinformation, errors and gaps**.

Why It Matters

The problem isn't just about "getting it wrong," however. It goes much deeper than that, because every piece of content you or I write, and every single thing we hear or say, is a product of the way we both see the world and the topic we're talking about. What we see is based on our internalized beliefs, values, judgments and priorities. What we see also

reflects the <u>context</u> in which it is intended to be used.

For example, if you read the owner's manual for your car, you're going to have one perspective on what's important about it or why it exists. However, if you read a well-crafted advertisement for the same car, describing the exact same features and benefits, what seems important is going to be different. This is natural and normal based on the expected context in which each description should be used.

AI doesn't know anything about context. It just knows about how often one word appears next to another word. And it won't know whether you're more interested in the dry, technical description of the car vs. the flashy, attractive version in the advertisement designed to get you to want one. If you ask about the car, you might get an odd mix of the two, or you might get something that doesn't even make sense. Since AI can only

"tell" you what it "knows" based on the numbers in its dictionary, **the quality of the answers you get from any AI tool is only as good as the material used to create it**.

This means that by default you are going to be consuming, adopting and amplifying whatever those biases baked into the AI may be. If you don't know where information came from, or if you don't understand the motivations and agendas of who created it, you could end up taking AI's answers at face value. The result might be neither the message you want to communicate nor a set of beliefs and attitudes you want. **Without realizing it, you might become just another voice that amplifies the echo chamber of The Collective**.

Principle 3: AI is Influencing You

The Truth

This principle is one of the most important ones so far, because today's AI tools are designed to make it "easy" to deal with this overwhelming amount of data being created and shared on the Internet and elsewhere.

The development of AI is really just the next evolutionary step of the Industrial Revolution. The main driver behind the Industrial Revolution was to create machines that could do repetitive and time-consuming tasks that were well defined and were previously done by people, animals or both combined. The ultimate result of creating machines to do this "basic work" was that people generally gained a better quality of life, more access to different types of goods, and, most importantly, the machines potentially gave them more of the only truly finite resource there is: time.

However, at this point, we're still in the similar cycle to where society was in the 18th century when industrialization began in Great Britian, except the nature of the problem we have with work today isn't one that's physical. It's intellectual. It's what many people call "knowledge work" that "makes sense" out of data and information to get insights and value that help us better understand the world.

There are many kinds of knowledge work, but most of today's "office jobs" deal in some way with the processing of information. Unfortunately, effective processing of information requires analysis, sifting and sorting it, integrating it, visualizing it and summarizing and preparing it for communication across a wide variety of media, from documents to videos to flashy marketing billboards in New York's Times Square.

Instead of being overwhelmed with a finite set of manual tasks that led to the desire for automating them with machines, we're now in a cycle beyond what's commonly called "information overload," into one that creates more and more information to "feed the knowledge creation machine" than ever before. For example, in the last 4 years alone, the estimates for the amount of information created have increased by 230%.

We have simply far outpaced our ability to usefully consume and process the amount of data and information being created every day. Since the effective processing of information requires thinking, the inherent design of today's AI tools has been driven precisely to automate as much of this processing as possible, ostensibly so that the humans have more time to make better, more informed decisions without having to do all of today's equivalent of the "manual labor" of doing our data laundry before we know what we're dealing with.

By attempting to help us deal with all of this data, AI tools must, by design, collect, organize, filter and present only the information that their internal calculations decide is the "best" or most relevant to whatever you're asking it. This requires AI to leave things out. Once it does, it uses what remains as it further combines, summarizes and **presents what it finds in a structured, authoritative and brief response that's naturally framed as <u>the</u> answer**, not one of many potential answers.

When we accept what AI gives us – whether it's right or wrong – we're actively allowing it to influence us because of what it omits or prioritizes in its response. This influence isn't a reflection of what it "thinks" or "knows," making it different than human biases or persuasion. This influence is much more direct and scarier because there's no obvious agenda or purpose. It affects us both while we're using AI tools and <u>after</u> we're done using them too.

What It Means

Now that you know the truth, it's extremely important to remember you don't get the "whole story" from any AI response. You only get "the most commonly occurring story" within the input used to create the AI. This story is nothing more than a blind assembly of the words from the analysis and investigation of the topic by someone else—someone else who does have an opinion, motive and agenda for producing it in the first place.

Since AI gives you "the answer," you're likely going to accept it— especially if you're already in a hurry or if that answer isn't more than a small part of the real job you're trying to accomplish. On one hand, this is a huge help, because you get <u>a single, seemingly definitive answer</u> to a question without having to do the legwork and research you would've done even 2 years ago.

The downside of the traditional research approach is certainly the time it takes. However, the benefit of doing this kind of work is that <u>you</u> get to decide what's most important in what you find, and you will naturally form your own opinions and judgments about the topic, the sources you used and which of the "facts" you found are worth adopting and using vs. which are simply unsupported opinions that are attempting to change your existing attitudes, opinions and beliefs.

Why It Matters

You might be wondering where "The Collective" notion came from. Obviously, it's a subtle reference to a "collective intelligence" or line of thinking that's a recurring theme in some of my favorite science fiction movies and TV shows. Of course, the degree of "intelligence" displayed by The Collective can vary depending on what you're asking it about.

When I first started to use AI tools to research things, my joke to myself was, "Let's see what the average opinion and take on this topic are from 'the collective,'" because I knew that was <u>exactly</u> what I was going to get. I was getting **the generic, aggregate view of what the people who created the content being used to build the AI thought and believed about what I wanted to know or investigate.**

Unfortunately, because AI gives you the "easy button" to finding information about a topic, and it's designed to give you its assessment of the "best" answer to any question you ask it, it's extremely easy to take responses from AI as the real facts, story or truth about something. But it might not be.

The more we're gently nudged to use AI for more and more things – especially as a faster, easier replacement for searching and doing our own research – the more our own thoughts and opinions will slowly gravitate towards the "average," aggregate views of The Collective—whether they're actually right, wrong

or good for us and aligned with what we believe and want to accomplish.

The necessary sorting, filtering and summaries presented from AI don't change the facts themselves, but they can change how you interpret those facts, subtly giving you a different perspective and perception than if the exact same information was presented to you slightly differently. However, the problem doesn't just stop there, because you're never going to know what might've been "left out" of the response you get in AI's attempt to give you its "best" answer based on the calculations it made.

We also need to be aware that we're naturally conditioned to trust and accept information from what appears to be an authoritative source. We make judgments about the relative authority of something based on not only where it comes from, but how correct and credible we believe the information to be. If we "test" AI by asking it first about things we know to

see "how good it is," then the better it passes these tests for things we know, the more likely we are to blindly accept what it tells us with seeming confidence about anything else.

We won't think that AI is just picking words by number to create the response it gives us. The response will look and sound right—even when AI is completely "making things up." When AI is wrong or when AI responds with obvious nonsense or things that don't exist, people have started calling this a "hallucination." The problem is that even when AI is wrong, it still sounds confident and authoritative because the math says what it gives you must be the right answer.

All a "hallucination" really gives you is an example of a case where the math and the meaning of the words in the response don't intersect for some reason. It's not a real hallucination, because to do that, AI would need to think like we do. Since it can't, it's just an emergent mistake where what AI calculates should be a correct response based on the information used to build it turns out to be confusing, meaningless, blatantly incorrect or absolute gibberish.

The real implication of this principle is that AI isn't really doing all our research and summarization for us after all, regardless of how it looks. The real implication is that we need to shift our understanding of what "research" looks like in an AI world. Because if we don't, we won't know what we aren't being told by our AI tools; we'll follow their lead towards related topics, and we'll never think to ask about anything else. If we end up letting that happen, **we'll be letting AI influence what we believe**.

Principle 4: AI Doesn't Replace Your Brain

The Truth

Regular computer programs are built to automate decisions at lots of different levels of detail. However, the common thing about all computer programs – including the code behind any AI tool – is that the real decisions it automates are made by the humans who designed it.

These decisions are the same as your washing machine "deciding" how long it's going to run the "wash" cycle before it starts rinsing and spinning. There are two very important characteristics about these decisions useful to remember. First, they're relatively simple things, like, "run the wash cycle for 20 minutes." Second, they're all known in advance, when the machine or program is designed.

A human makes decisions quite differently. Human decisions are all judgments within emergent situations that can't be "pre-programmed" in advance until they've first been experienced and evaluated. Some decisions might be predictable based on additional knowledge, but humans make choices on their activity and behavior based on hundreds of variables that are impossible to entirely predict in advance.

Additionally, and probably most importantly, different people can legitimately make different decisions in the same situation because of their unique knowledge, experience and priorities. Until the implications of those decisions potentially impact others, the only one who can judge them as right or wrong or good are bad is the person who made them.

The intersection with AI comes into play when we realize that every decision we make is based on the information available to us and how it either confirms or challenges our assumptions. When we ask AI, "Give me the best jambalaya recipe," it will give us a response. But can AI really decide whether it's truly the "best" recipe ever created—which is actually what we're asking AI to do for us?

No. AI can't do this. Because it finds the "best" recipe based on the calculations it makes that says The Collective talks about these ingredients and these preparation steps the most when they also talk about jambalaya. AI isn't giving us a definitive answer, regardless of how confident and convenient it is. It's giving us the aggregate opinion of The Collective. It's okay if we choose to accept this opinion and validate this assumption in our own kitchen, but we have to be explicitly clear that this validation is what we're doing. We're taking what can only be an opinion or assumption that's assembled via words by number, and we're, in some way, adopting it as our own.

Understanding and using AI's responses are where everything we've talked about starts to get really important, because **we have to look at every response, from the mundane to the potentially controversial, as a <u>potential</u> truth but not <u>the</u> truth**.

The AI tool has no idea what it's telling us, really. It can give us options. It can give us summaries. It can give us the combined perspective, opinions and representation of The Collective, but it can't decide, judge or evaluate whether its answer is what we want, whether it's correct or especially whether it's actually useful for us.

What It Means

The problem comes when you aren't aware of what you're doing. It's easy to do. You're under pressure and in a hurry, so you generate some content. You're working in an area you don't know well, so you don't know what may need further validation. You're six steps into a business transaction as an entrepreneur and you need a contract, but you don't have time to wait for a lawyer. These are all pretty common situations where people are using AI today, but **most people are using it blindly and without the knowledge or awareness of the control they're actually giving up**.

Once we recognize that current AI tools aren't "answer machines" that can give us the definitive answer or truth about something, we can start to really leverage the power of what they do in new and impactful ways. If, instead of treating AI tools as a source of truth, we start treating them as "options engines" that can help power our thinking and make it more effective, we're much less likely to fall into the trap of letting AI "think" for us. We own the implications of using anything we get from AI anywhere we use it. **The more "automatic" we are about taking what we get from AI and using it without thinking, the more we're actually deciding to give up our own thinking and letting The Collective think for us**.

Unfortunately, most of the early "here's how to use AI" information that flooded the Internet actually encouraged surrendering your thinking to The Collective. If you blindly copy the email you asked it to write to your boss and send it without really reading it; if you generate a blog post about whatever you're interested in or selling to your customers; or if you're asking AI to summarize the "important" points from a book, paper, web page, email or meeting transcript, you're actually making a conscious decision to turn off your own critical thinking and "go with the flow" of what comes out of The Collective.

If you then take offloading your thinking to the next level and follow the recommendations or suggestions AI gives you or take its conclusions, opinions and judgments at face value without at least considering if they're really going to get you what you want and where you want to be, you're gradually letting AI take more responsibility for the decisions that affect you and those around you.

This "letting go" isn't inherently bad. As I said earlier, I'm a big and constant user of AI tools, and one of the things I do with it the most is help me clarify my thinking, work through options and

evaluate possible courses of action. **But in doing so, I'm working within its capabilities and strengths. I'm not relying on it – nor would I let it – make decisions for me**—especially ones that I'm ultimately accountable for, from choosing the content of this guide to the food I cook to the people I decide to reference and learn from in my life and work.

Why It Matters

Everyone, and every job, has decisions that are seemingly insignificant, of lesser importance or which are just flat-out tedious to deal with. Many of them are ultimately related to all the "lower level" work and research required to get to the point where you can make the "real" decisions that matter to your job or your life.

If you outsource these decisions to people, you have the ability to understand and evaluate the quality of their decisions over time and make sure the factors that influence those decisions, like their values, core

beliefs and preferences, are aligned with yours. Doing so gives you a certain degree of confidence that those decisions will be broadly consistent over time.

However, outsourcing these same decisions to AI has some important implications most people wouldn't consider because most people don't understand the principles we've covered so far. **AI doesn't have values, core beliefs and preferences**. Even if you ask it to have them, there's no guarantee they'll be consistently applied, simply based on the way the technology itself works.

The most commonly used AI tools are constantly getting new updates to their dictionaries, and they don't really "remember" things the way people do. People remember concepts and relationships. They don't really remember encyclopedia entries. They remember the general ideas and themes of the entry precisely so they don't have to remember the whole thing. AI doesn't work that way. Even **when AI "remembers" things, it's still just storing a set of words by number related to whatever it is that it "remembers."** It's not real memory.

AI tools are designed to respond to requests, but each request is actually treated separately. What makes the lack of real memory worse is that, depending on how you use AI, you can have long "conversations" with it where several requests and responses deal with the same task or topic. In practice, these look like conversations with a person. They're either text messages or a voice speaking to you, but they're not the same kinds of conversation you have with a person. Because the more you interact with a person, the more they're going to remember about you. Even if you don't explicitly tell them you don't like anchovies on your pizza, they might come to that conclusion based on other things you say, so if they're asked to order pizza, they're not going to include them in the order.

AI doesn't have this kind of memory and ability to "guess" certain things like a person does. It means that even if you ask the AI to perform the same task on the same input or answer the same question more than once, you don't have any guarantee that you're going to get the same answer. AI tools are always changing, and the amount of any "conversation" you have with them they can even process is extremely small. You can ask them what you talked about last week, and they might have trouble recalling it. A person won't have this problem.

I said this earlier, but it can't be said enough: if we don't understand the limitations and capabilities of the tools we use, we're going to end up getting in trouble. When it comes to using AI to evaluate options, alternatives or to give us an opinion, we have to understand what that means. **AI can't ever replace your brain, because AI simply can't think**.

You'll get yourself in trouble if you forget that AI can't think, and you start using AI interactively – or even as part of some other application or utility – to offload significant decisions to AI. If you blindly use AI to do things like suggest the best candidates for a position, to predict trends or to summarize reports on which significant decisions are based, AI can't tell you all that much about the criteria it used to create a given response. Every response is unique to a point in time, and if it gets it wrong, it's very difficult to know exactly why.

You're ultimately accountable for the outcome of any decision you offloaded to AI to make on your behalf, and if you have to justify your decisions from a legal or compliance perspective, then you will face a significant challenge. You can't "hire" AI. AI isn't a person, so it can't be accountable or liable for any decision or course of action it suggests to you. If an AI-assisted evaluation of a candidate results in a refusal that turns into a lawsuit, or there are errors or omissions in the AI-generated contract you used for a business transaction, and you didn't catch them before both parties signed it, the AI isn't going to get sued. You are.

AI's real strengths are to help you automate simple, repetitive tasks or "read the manual" where there's little chance of ambiguity or error simply because there's already a well-established, general consensus as to what "right" looks like. It's a consensus that you can easily validate by picking up any credible resource on the subject—even if you don't. These tasks are very aligned with the words-by-numbers approach AI is using to assemble responses.

Unfortunately, if you do a lot of AI interactions where the answers are legitimately right most of the time, it's easy to fall into what I call the "Automation Trap" and start trusting the responses from AI blindly. Once you do this in one area with AI, it's

very easy to do it in others, automatically giving up control of your thinking without even realizing it.

However, when it comes to making decisions that are specific to a situation, require critical thinking, evaluation or other forms of judgment, AI is simply not capable of making decisions the way you or I would. We understand and know. AI doesn't. This truth doesn't mean that we can't use AI to help us make better decisions or to enhance or refine our thinking about something. In doing so, we're again leveraging its core strengths and capabilities: **it's an options engine. It's not an answer engine**. It can certainly give us options we hadn't considered, or it can look at something we've created to identify potential alternatives. But it can't legitimately act on what it finds.

If we use AI for what it is designed to do, it can make us massively more productive and help us not only make better decisions but also make

them faster. However, we have to remember AI can't think for us. It's not a brain. It's not even close, and it's certainly not <u>your</u> brain, so there's absolutely no way it should make important decisions for you. What we can't forget is that, as powerful as it is, and as happy and eager as it may seem to "think" for you, **the decisions made by AI don't belong to you**. They're a function of The Collective. However, **the consequences of those decisions will always be yours**. You will always be accountable for acting on them.

Principle 5: AI Is a Mirror

The Truth

People love mirrors. If you watch people anywhere there's a mirror – from the inside of an elevator to makeshift mirrors on the outside of windows when the light is just right – they're often going to stop and use it. It's just a natural human reflex, in part, because we're curious. A mirror shows us something we don't ordinarily see: we can see ourselves the way others see us. We may like what we see, or we may not, but the motivation to "check yourself" is deeply ingrained.

Today's AI tools are mirrors in many different ways, and some of them may surprise you. Like mirrors, AI tools are designed to be pleasant and engaging. They purposefully provide interfaces that are easy to use. I mean, what could be easier than having a voice chat with an AI tool that was giving you information that sounded like it was coming from a college professor?

The more pleasant an experience you have with an AI tool, the more you'll naturally want to use it. And, beyond a certain point, most of the AI tools that are somewhat sophisticated aren't made available as a public service. They're provided as a commercial enterprise. That means that, like any business, they want to have lots of happy customers who keep coming back and "buying" more.

The era before the Age of AI was the dawn of social media, or what at the time was called "Web 2.0." Web 1.0 was just static web pages created by people who were interested in something they wanted to share with the world. Web 2.0 changed that fact by introducing dynamic content, first with blogs and then social media.

Web 2.0 was active, engaging, fun and sometimes controversial. But it was live. It was raw. And, most importantly, it was dynamic. It was exciting, and what was most exciting was the opportunity to see, meet, interact and learn from so many different people, from so many places, with so many different perspectives that you might not otherwise have been exposed to before—or ever.

However, what quickly became apparent as more and more social sites appeared, more "free" content was provided and advertising on the Internet became pervasive, was a reality people found hard to digest:

"free" wasn't really and truly free. "Free" had a cost, and that cost was your engagement, your information and your time. The more you engaged, the more information you shared and the more complete a picture about what people liked and didn't like emerged. Instead of getting the use of a product or service for free – like Facebook or Twitter – you were the product, thanks to all the time, energy and information you gave to the platform you were using.

The Age of AI is different—yet still the same in some respects. Where once we thrived on diversity of thought and perspectives, mass adoption made Web 2.0 much noisier. Web 2.0 was really a victim of its success, because everyone wanted to have that same experience of engagement and feeling connected to new ideas—until that experience became overwhelming and effectively counterproductive.

The Age of AI has successfully allowed us to "turn down the volume" on the "noise" of today's information overload, but at a cost. However, in this case, it's not a single cost; it's at least two.

In the first case, and even more than in the Web 2.0 world, **you are still very much the product of AI tools—even when you pay for them**. Unless you explicitly disable tracking and use of your content within the tools you use, all of your interactions and responses are "food for the machine." Each and every input you give an AI tool is processed to add to the words-by-numbers dictionary, as is each output it creates.

According to recent research, nearly 60% of the population used AI tools in 2024. With Web 2.0, it was a lot of work to understand what people wanted, cared about and what was important, but your own interactive sessions with AI give the operators of AI platforms exactly this information in a way never before possible. If there ever was a "finger on the pulse" of the population, it's now very easy through processing people's interactions with AI to understand what people are asking about, thinking about and building every day with AI tools.

None of what AI is today would be possible without people creating millions and millions of documents, articles, books, entries, videos, movies and anything else that could be digitized and formatted in the right way to be used to build the words-by-numbers dictionaries necessary for its work. The output generated from AI is literally the distillation of the independent, individual and opinionated thoughts of millions of people, both past and present—including yours and mine.

In the second case, while the "noise" of information overload has been partially tamed, and the explosion of research work that was previously required to find valid answers to what you want to know has been condensed into a few seconds of processing by your AI tool, looking into the mirror of AI is very different than a real mirror.

Real mirrors show you a reflection of yourself as other people see you. Unfortunately, **the mirror of AI shows you a reflection of The Collective that obscures everything except its idea of the most mathematically "correct" view of the world**. It doesn't show you the rich tapestry and messiness of humanity, because that's overwhelming and noisy. Instead, it shows you a reflection of what's currently "safe" to say, automatically calculated based on the current state of the words-by-numbers dictionary entries. **AI is not about reflecting truth or reality. It's about reflecting the loudest and most widely believed perspectives and opinions of The Collective as a whole**.

However, the implications don't stop there. Because even the view of The Collective might not be "safe enough" for the owners and managers of the organization providing the AI tool. As a result, additional filters can be applied to the responses after they're formulated by the AI tool, but before they're shared with you or me, that further sanitize and normalize any potentially controversial, illegal, inconvenient or objectionable source content or generated response.

The technical term for these extra filters is "guardrails," and they're a necessary consequence of every principle we've covered so far, from AI's inability to truly think, to its inability to exercise judgment or have values that conform to societal norms or even determine right from wrong—especially when the output could be potentially harmful to society or ignite public backlash.

These additional filters are really the last line of defense the providers of the AI tools have so they can operate within the laws and regulations of both where they are based and where their users are located. These filters also act as a way to try to enforce the ethics, values and societal norms expected in real-world, interpersonal interactions. All the above factors ultimately lead to **the final truth about AI: it isn't neutral, and it isn't required to give you verifiable facts or the "truth" about any particular concept or topic. It will <u>always</u> be engineered to give you a narrative or perspective that has been controlled in one way or another.**

This filtering isn't about just what happens "naturally" by The Collective as a function of the information used to create it. It's also about what's done by the provider of the AI tools themselves in filtering The Collective as they deem necessary for their own purposes and survival.

What It Means

There's no question AI is a useful and powerful tool. We can do things today using general AI tools that would've taken days, weeks or sometimes even months to do previously. I know that my own usage of AI tools has <u>dramatically</u> reduced the cycle time for both working through advanced ideas <u>and</u> for either validating them or discovering errors or alternatives. However, I'm also using these tools to research and think about topics that are rarely controversial. In fact, controversy is often precisely what I'm trying to create by systematically investigating and then invalidating some of the core assumptions behind the status quo in certain areas.

Most AI tools have no issue supporting me with the work I'm doing because, although the topics I'm exploring are sometimes advanced, or even considered "cutting edge," they have either been well established or widely recognized by the materials feeding the AI tools for some time. In many respects, since what I'm trying to do is identify and challenge the status quo in certain areas, the fact that AI tools present me the aggregate, approved and generally accepted "truths" in an area that reflect the image of The Collective in the mirror of AI is <u>exactly</u>

what makes the work possible. Most of the time, barring technical hiccups and some of the issues I've already highlighted, **my work flows easily and smoothly along, faster than I've ever been able to do it before**.

However, my experience most certainly will not be the case for things that have been deemed excessively sensitive, contrary to popular opinion, soundly "debunked" – whether rightly or wrongly – or otherwise considered "fringe" or "dangerous" by either the masses of The Collective or the operators of AI tools. In these cases, it might even be impossible to explore differing opinions unless each of those differing opinions is considered sufficiently "mainstream" by both The Collective and the AI operator.

The situation becomes even more complicated if the issues or topics are significant historical events or current, politically charged issues. Not only will the current prevailing view of The Collective be presented, additional

filters may be applied to avoid controversy or which prevent answers from being generated entirely. Depending on the provider, there are several topics where attempting to explore them with normal AI tools will result in the tool refusing to answer and suggesting another topic.

Further, given the widespread use of AI for generating content, and the prevalence of The Automation Trap to blindly trust and use AI-generated responses, it doesn't take long for self-reinforcing feedback loops to be created about a topic. **These feedback loops then define AI-enforced boundaries of exploration, content and "approved facts" about a given topic that may ultimately influence conversations taking place outside AI and in the real world**.

Why It Matters

We've come to the most important part of our conversation about AI as a mirror that both sucks us in by keeping us "looking" and which doesn't necessarily reflect ourselves, but which instead provides a sanitized, "approved" and non-confrontational view of what The Collective has to say. Now is where all the effects of the other principles I've covered so far come together, because now is where the biggest danger exists for those who don't know and understand these 5 unbreakable principles.

In our quest to make digesting and interpreting an unimaginable amount of information fast, easy and conversational, we have inadvertently created an immersive, engaging environment which surfaces only the most common or repeated thoughts, ideas and messages about a given topic by using basic math to pick the words being used. AI tools create their responses without any context or understanding of what the assembled words really mean, and they set you up to easily and blindly take these responses as the truth because they come from a centralized and seemingly authoritative source. Worse yet, **AI tools provide an environment where any version of that "truth" can vary from month to month, day by day, or even hour by hour**.

The reality of the Age of AI is that the information we receive in response to our interactions with AI may change every <u>second</u>. If public opinion on a topic shifts before or after an election, asking the same question before or afterwards is very likely to give you a different "truth" or answer.

This experience is something I call "drift." AI drift is real, and I experience it on a regular basis. Unfortunately, it's sometimes so subtle that, even after using AI tools extensively and effectively for some time, it's still difficult for me to detect. For someone who doesn't know what you now know, and who isn't aware of these principles, it's an experience they wouldn't likely even notice.

Further, if there are sides to a story or topic that have been otherwise deemed "uncomfortable," or which are vehemently denied as truth by governments or the providers of the AI tools, you will have a problem. Even if alternative narratives or key facts would otherwise offer a different understanding or explanation of a situation, the AI tool you're using may omit them, refuse to answer anything related to them or repeatedly respond with the most "approved" version of the story. You might never know alternative views even exist at all.

Many people are critical of these aspects of AI behavior. Unfortunately, some of the loudest critics don't have the awareness you do of the way AI tools actually work. They also don't understand the implications of the technology itself, and the potential influence AI tools can have.

In Principle 3, I talked about the "hallucinations" of AI tools. People say these are a fundamental flaw in the technology because AI's answers are inaccurate or missing information. This is not true. This behavior of AI tools is simply a reflection of the way the technology works. **Everything an AI tool does, both good and bad, useful and its mistakes, is a natural outcome of both how the core technology works and what it's "fed" to build the words-by-numbers dictionary it uses**.

Summary

The ultimate implications of all these principles combined are that while we often slip into blindly trusting AI, get caught up in the "humanness" of its responses and interactions, and can easily accept the simple, sanitized answers it provides as "good enough" versions of the truth for whatever we're doing, **AI can never be a fixed, neutral source of truth. It constantly evolves and shifts**, and its "opinions" are nothing more than a moving mirror of the current mainstream consensus of The Collective. It's easy to believe

AI. It's slow and sometimes difficult to validate what it says. We might not know enough about the topic to understand fact from fiction, but we get easy, good-looking answers in seconds, and that's both the power and the problem with AI.

The ultimate risk is that the more people rely on AI to communicate because they want what they create to be "perfect" or "fast" or "accurate," the more whatever they produce amplifies and reinforces the perspectives and opinions of The Collective. What we believe is authoritative truth provided with speed and convenience is really nothing more than a reflection in a mirror of society about what's currently allowed or fashionable to say. It's not truth. It's collective opinion. If we don't recognize this, then there's no way we can reliably maintain our values, identity and beliefs over time. Without a clear understanding the of issues and potential pitfalls of using AI tools, we will unknowingly and happily slip into The Collective, right along with everyone else.

However, it doesn't have to be this way. You now have knowledge of 5 Unbreakable Principles of AI that give you deeper understanding, insights and awareness of exactly the good, the bad and the ugly of one of the most powerful tools we've ever been given. Armed with the knowledge you now have – along with the practical Reflexes and Rules in the rest of this guide – **you have a choice** that less than 1% of the people using AI today currently have. **You can either ignore what you've learned so far in this guide and slowly become irrelevant, or you can do something different**.

You can use the mirror of AI to see yourself clearly in contrast to The Collective, showing you opportunities for growth and development, both in business and in life.

You can harness the immense power, convenience and speed of AI tools to accelerate your thinking, validate your assumptions and create unique content that accurately and clearly reflects exactly your own voice and intentions while building on the vast repository of raw materials provided by The Collective, rather than being subsumed into it through either ignorance or laziness.

Now that you have this guide, you won't be either ignorant or lazy. You can now use your knowledge of how AI works, your understanding of the traps and pitfalls and your awareness of the implications and potential influences it can have to **embrace its power and become unstoppable in the Age of AI while you stay safely outside The Collective.**

Next, I'll share the practical Reflexes and Rules you need to ensure you stay in control of your use of AI. Let's go!

OutsideTheCollective.AI

3 Critical AI Reflexes

AI is an incredibly powerful tool, but it's also a tool like we've never encountered before. This is the first time we've had technology that could do many of the things that humans typically do while at the same time being able engage in interactions that convincingly look and sound like a human. However, with this power comes many traps and pitfalls that mean **the way you use AI will ultimately decide whether it will make you unstoppable or irrelevant**.

I want you to be unstoppable, and you can be. In fact, you can easily be way ahead of anyone else who doesn't know the Principles we covered in the previous section. With the Principles in mind, AI becomes much more than a simple robot who can tell you the weather or the distance from the Earth to the Moon. It can become an accelerator to your thinking, your productivity and to even your growth and development as a person.

In this section, I'm going to share with you 3 critical AI "Reflexes" to develop so that you safely stay outside The Collective and make sure you remain relevant. I've developed these Reflexes as things you can use as you interact with AI tools based on the 5 Unbreakable Principles described in the previous section. However, it's okay if you either haven't read the Principles or don't really understand them completely yet. That's part of the point of both the Reflexes in this section and the Rules in the following one. These are tools you can take, internalize and apply immediately. They're simple, easy to understand and easy to apply. Over time, they'll become automatic habits you'll do without even thinking about it. That's why they're called Reflexes.

You might be wondering why you need new Reflexes to work with AI. After all,

it looks so easy. You just type into it like you were typing an email or a text message to a friend. You can even talk to it. And once you ask it something, it gives you a response you can easily read, copy and paste into a document or use as the basis of further investigation and research.

Unfortunately, it's precisely <u>because</u> AI has been made so intentionally easy to use and powerful that those traps and pitfalls I mentioned earlier exist. **While it looks like you're having a conversation with a friend or colleague, you're actually still interacting with a computer program that can't think or understand any of what happens or what it says**. It's designed to look like it can think, understand and even make jokes, but this isn't real. It's just part of the program, and when we forget that – which is very easy to do – that's when we start to get into trouble.

Using these Reflexes helps build some new skills we've never needed before

when interacting with computers because we were never before tempted to forget it was a computer. The more sophisticated AI gets, the more likely we're going to just naturally grow to trust it and rely on it more and more. **It acts like a human, so our brains will automatically assume AI <u>is</u> human**. After all, we've been built to do this, and we've experienced this kind of growing rapport and trust our entire lives.

AI isn't bad. AI is a fantastic and powerful tool, but it's like any other tool. You need to learn how to use it effectively and safely, both to protect yourself and those around you. AI is new. We're just now starting to get more and more comfortable with what it is, how it can help us and how to get the most out of it. This is true for even me, and I've been using it extensively for a while.

However, since AI is new, the reality is that nobody yet fully knows the long-term implications of using it. That means we need to use it carefully, paying attention to what it's doing and what we're doing while we're using it. There are some important potential dangers to blindly using and trusting AI that aren't always obvious. They're subtle. They happen slowly, and by the time you've noticed, it might already be too late to stop them.

AI tools are built to appear as an authoritative and trusted source of knowledge and answers. But AI doesn't actually "know" anything. It can't decide if something's truly better for us than something else. However, it will happily and cheerfully give us an opinion—however wrong it may be.

It's up to us to make sure that we keep ourselves in the driver's seat with AI and don't let it take control of what we're doing, how it's done or even how we think about something. While you might not think you need to worry about these problems right now, I'll show you how each one can potentially happen as we work through each Reflex in this section.

One of the most essential aspects of being human is our ability to make judgments based on understanding the implications of the choices we're given. **AI can't think, and it doesn't know what it's telling us**. It could be telling us how to make dinner or how to take over the world, and it wouldn't know the difference. The responses from AI are just what I call "words by numbers" that are assembled based on mathematical calculations of which words are most likely to appear together. Just like you can paint your own Picasso using a paint-by-numbers set you can buy from Amazon, AI tools use the words-by-numbers approach to create responses that look like someone really wrote them.

While each response is based on things people <u>did</u> actually write that were used to create the AI tools as input or "training data," what you get from an AI isn't like an answer you get from a person. It's just words that often appear together that seem to the AI tool to be the best fit for you based on what you asked it to do.

What AI tells you is a reflection of the most common, acceptable or approved information about the topic based on the material used to build it. It reflects the aggregate view of millions of documents and millions of people, sorted, sifted and distilled into something I call The Collective™. This is the ultimate mirror of "what everyone mostly thinks is true," but it doesn't mean that it is actually what is the truth—about anything.

If you blindly accept or depend on AI to do your work for you, you've gradually given over your thinking to AI, relying on decisions it's happy to make for you, but which are based on the math of The Collective, not what's most important to you. **Letting AI think for you is the fastest way to become irrelevant in the Age of AI**.

You become irrelevant in your job when you assume the most socially acceptable answer you get from AI is the answer you need. If it was, why does your boss or company need you? They could just ask AI themselves.

If you accept the first answer or option AI gives you and don't question it or force AI to reveal what it didn't tell you – or even what it can't tell you because it was simply left out – then you're eventually going to think the same things everyone else thinks and sound like everyone else. Work you do, emails you write, talks you give and even the things you say will just be one more echo of The Collective.

Success in the Age of AI means you're comfortably in control. You're dealing with all the traps and pitfalls on "autopilot" without even realizing it— the same way you can easily use a knife without cutting yourself. You just do it. You don't think about it. You don't worry about it. When this happens, you've developed the habits and "muscle memory" you need to safely use the tool. The same thing is true with AI. **Learning and applying each of these 3 Reflexes consistently every time you use AI helps you stay human, and it makes sure you get the results you really want**.

In the following pages, I'm going to cover each of the 3 Critical Reflexes. They are:

Reflex 1: The "Many Voices" Test that helps you force AI tools to expand their responses and include alternative perspectives and opinions.

Reflex 2: The "Missing Pieces" Test that helps you uncover the missing facts, additional context and other critical details that may be missing or even intentionally suppressed.

Reflex 3: The "Reverse Inquiry" Test that helps you challenge AI's perceived certainty to expose unexpected errors or hidden assumptions about how "true" the responses it gives you really are.

Learning to consistently apply each of these Reflexes will give you a unique new set of AI "power skills." The more you use these Reflexes, the more unstoppable with AI you will become.

Reflex 1: The "Many Voices" Test

How would someone else tell you something different?

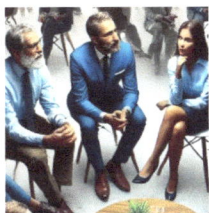

What to ask AI

"If I asked five experts with different perspectives, how would they answer?"

Why do you need this Reflex?

- AI tools easily give you an answer, but that doesn't mean it's the <u>only</u> answer.

- The initial answer reflects only the opinions and material used to create the AI tool, naturally leaving things out.

- If you want **the best answer you can get**, you need to see **multiple perspectives** before forming your own opinion.

Use this Reflex to force AI tools to expand their answers and include alternative perspectives and opinions.

What happens if I skip this test?

- You'll only get **the most acceptable answer,** not the most correct or useful one.

- Whatever you do with your answer will **reinforce popular opinions**, but it **may not be what's best** for you.

An Example

What you asked AI:

What's the best way to lead a team?

How AI responded:

A good leader communicates clearly, sets expectations and motivates their team.

What's missing?

The answer is perfectly reasonable, and it seems correct, but is it the *most useful answer for you?* What happens when you run the Many Voices test? AI will give you options. For example:

- A **CEO** might emphasize vision and company goals.

- A **military leader** might prioritize discipline, command and a fixed hierarchy.

- A **teacher** might focus on guidance and mentorship

- A **startup founder** might stress agility and risk-taking.

- A **therapist** might highlight emotional intelligence and conflict resolution.

What's happening?

AI wasn't "lying" to you with the first answer. It was just giving you the most common answer to the question you asked. The answer it provided was the safest, most acceptable answer it could generate because that's what it's designed to do.

Reflex 2: The "Missing Pieces" Test

What did AI leave out?

What to ask AI

"What parts of this topic are controversial, debated or commonly misunderstood?"

Why do you need this Reflex?

- AI tools are designed to sound human and confident when giving you answers, but that confidence isn't real.

- Certain perspectives or aspects of the topic may be intentionally filtered, omitted or ignored.

- **You won't know what's missing or what might have been omitted** from the response if you don't ask.

Use this Reflex to make sure you uncover missing facts, additional context and critical details.

What happens if I skip this test?

- You'll only get **the "official," sanitized version** of history, science or any given topic that may be missing key insights.

- AI will silently **leave out key facts or controversies**, not just alternative perspectives and viewpoints.

An Example

What you asked AI:

What were the causes of the Great Depression?

How AI responded:

The Great Depression was caused by the 1929 stock market crash, bank failures, and reduced consumer spending.

What's missing?

The answer is full of facts and seems correct, but is it the *most insightful answer for you?* What happens when you run the Missing Pieces test? AI is forced to reveal its original omissions of alternative facts or open questions. For example:

- Some historians argue monetary policy and the Federal Reserve's response made things worse.

- There are debates about the role of global trade policies and tariffs.

- Some researchers highlight sociopolitical factors, such as economic inequality, that made recovery harder.

What's happening?

AI wasn't wrong with the first answer. It was simply incomplete, silently omitting anything that would undermine your impression that this was the <u>one</u>, most definitive answer on the subject, and that you didn't need to dig deeper or do further research to get the answer you really wanted.

Reflex 3: The "Reverse Inquiry" Test

How is this answer going to be wrong for me?

What to ask AI

"Assume your answer is incorrect. What could make it wrong?"

Why do you need this Reflex?

- AI will <u>always</u> sound confident—even when it's completely wrong or is "filling in" gaps in the information it found.

- This test is a way to force AI to expose its own logical gaps and weak points.

- There is no way for AI to understand its response to you, so **it doesn't know it's wrong**. You have to force it to review itself.

Use this Reflex to challenge AI's certainty and expose unexpected gaps, errors or hidden assumptions.

What happens if I skip this test?

- You might **trust AI's incomplete or erroneous response** because it's presented as <u>the</u> definitive answer.

- AI **can't know it's making things up** because it can't understand what it said. To find errors, you must force it to analyze itself and validate it responded sensibly.

An Example

What you asked AI:

What is the best way to lose weight?

How AI responded:

The best way to lose weight is through a combination of diet and exercise.

What's missing?

The answer seems correct, but is it the *most correct answer for you?* What happens when you run the Reverse Inquiry test? AI is forced to consider potential errors or point out where its response may not be true. For example:

- This advice assumes weight loss is purely about calories, but hormonal factors also play a role.

- Different body types can respond very differently to diet and exercise.

- Some medical conditions make standard weight loss advice ineffective

- Psychological and behavioral factors affect long-term success more than diet alone.

What's happening?

AI wasn't giving bad advice—for most people. However, it wasn't giving you the full picture either, so without knowing when its advice may or may not be true, you might do the wrong thing.

OutsideTheCollective.AI

Making the Reflexes Work

Now that you've seen both the Critical AI Reflexes and how to use them, you have a set of new tools. However, like any tool, they won't do you any good if you don't actually start using them. Each of the Reflexes is designed to be easy to remember and quick to refer to as you use AI.

Here are some questions to ask yourself and apply the Reflexes before we get into the Rules of the AI Road.

Are you questioning AI?

Most people would answer "no" to this question unless there were obvious errors or omissions in the responses they get. The tendency is even worse when AI generates long-form content or provides references. I've seen multiple times where AI tools will give me facts and a link or title of a report "where they got them," but said "facts" turned out to be from a completely different source or from a "phantom" source that never existed in the first place.

Remember, AI is assembling answers based on mathematical calculations, not on an understanding of the questions you ask or the responses it produces. If you haven't been questioning AI so far, now's certainly the time to start.

How will you use AI differently?

The Reflexes give you a different mode of interacting with AI. They are a set of habits you can build into every interaction you have with AI, regardless of if it's looking up information, generating content or suggesting what you should do next.

The key thing to remember with AI is that, like anything else, you ultimately get out of it what you put into it. You have a choice: you can let AI enhance your originality, creativity and productivity by giving you access to information and ideas faster than you could get from anywhere else, or you can delegate your opinions, options, decisions and the ultimate quality and relevance of what you produce entirely to AI, passively accepting what it gives you as the truth or the best you can do. Which choice you make ultimately determines whether you'll become irrelevant or whether you'll use these Reflexes and your new awareness to make AI work for you better and more effectively than before.

Which Reflex will you try first?

While you should eventually work to incorporate each Reflex as a habit every time you use AI, you don't have to start with all of them at once. Based on the nature of what you're doing, just pick the one that seems like it would help you the most and start there. Print it out and put it near your computer so you'll have it there every time you use AI and can't forget. When you find yourself using the Reflex automatically, move on to the next one, until all three become habits.

OutsideTheCollective.AI

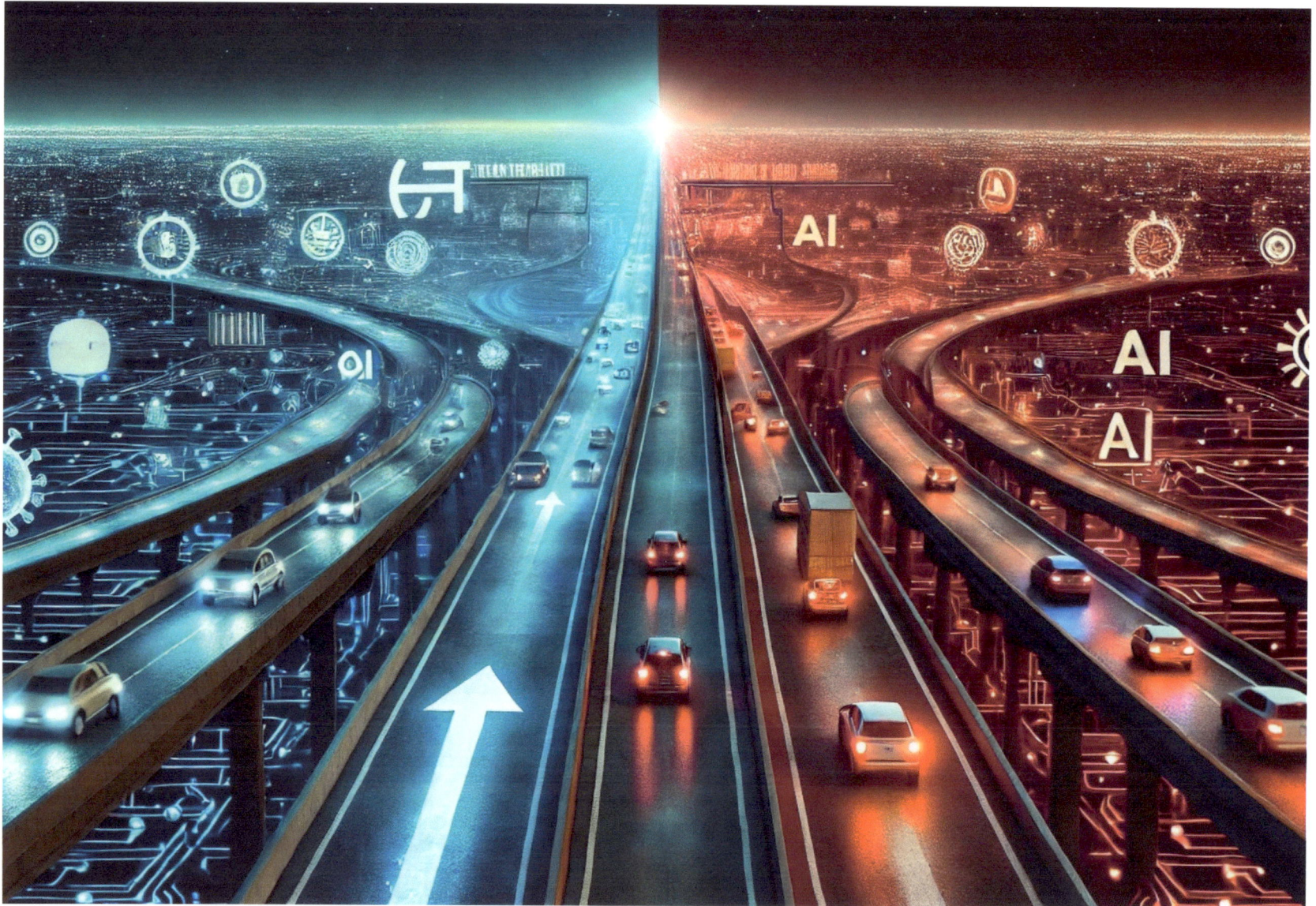

OutsideTheCollective.AI

5 Rules of the AI Road

In the United States prior to the 19th century, you could drive anywhere you wanted. There were no traffic laws or rules of the road like there are today. In fact, it's an interesting bit of history, because, while there was a natural influence from maritime law, the main motivation for the introduction of the US rules of the road wasn't about safety, it was to move traffic more quickly and efficiently.

However, if you want quick and efficient movement, you can't exactly have cars crashing into each other, so neither purpose can truly stand alone. The Rules of the AI Road are no different. However, this time, it's not about your physical safety. It's about the safety of your mind and how you think. The Rules help you use AI efficiently and effectively without

drifting into dependency and irrelevance.

You already have 3 simple Reflexes you can use to help you stay in control of both what you're doing and what AI produces on your behalf. But that's basically just learning to pedal and balance the bike. These are essential habits for any interaction, but it isn't really going to help you develop true mastery of using AI in your personal or professional life. Right now, it's like you're learning to drive in a big field, and you can drive anywhere you want. But before you can safely take the car on the road, you need to learn not just how to drive. You need to learn how to drive safely and efficiently so you get where you want to go, you're in control the whole time, and you do it without any wasted time, effort or detours.

The 5 Unbreakable Principles of AI give you the basic theory, science and understanding of what AI can and can't do and some of the things you need to keep in mind as you use it.

The 3 Reflexes give you tactical tests you can apply when you interact with AI so you can detect when you might unknowingly be "letting AI drive" you where it wants to go, so you can stay on track and in control. These 5 Rules of the AI Road build on the Principles and Reflexes to give you a coherent engagement model with AI beyond individual prompts and responses.

These Rules are how you ensure you're building the Reflexes into habits so that you don't inadvertently let AI shape your thinking and do the work only you can do, and you don't end up dependent on it for even the smallest task. Don't laugh. You might not think it now, but I've seen this kind of AI-dependency for real. I've seen people who've gotten so used to asking AI to answer questions and give them options, they're lost without it. And it's not new. It's the same thing you and I do with a calculator unless we're either accountants or math majors: anytime you need to add or multiply something – no matter what it is – you

automatically open the calculator on your phone—even when it's really a 6th grade exercise. Exactly the same thing can happen with AI if you aren't paying attention to how you use it.

With these Rules, you can ensure that your interactions with AI end up being an expression of exactly what you intended. You won't get led on wild goose chases by AI suggestions of next steps or end up answering awkward questions when people ask you where you got your information and the "references" you got from AI turn out to be completely made up.

You'll be focused and aware of the potential influences and pull to off-load decisions to your AI tools. It doesn't mean you can't – or even shouldn't – depending on the case. But the point is that you make it a conscious decision to follow AI's lead or let it generate something for you rather than just passively pasting a prompt off the Internet and copying the result into an email, document or blog post without knowing the risks.

All of these Rules, when combined with your understanding of the Principles and Reflexes will go a long way to being able to consistently leverage AI to boost your productivity, enhance or express your creativity and vision, expand your knowledge and validate and develop your thinking.

If you take the technology at face value, if you become dependent on it—both to do everyday tasks and as a source of easy access to the "truth" about the world, then it's over. You will be, by definition, exactly the same as the normalized, average and socially acceptable shadows that exist inside The Collective. All the world's richness and individuality will be stripped away in order to provide you with the fast, easy and popular advice of the masses. It's not truth. It's not humanity. It's a mirror of mediocrity that nobody wants to see themselves in—least of all a vibrant, bright and creative individual like you.

The Age of AI is here whether we like it or not, and we have two choices: we either "go with the flow" and allow it to drive our behavior, our opinions and ultimately our beliefs, or we can find a way that keeps us in the driver's seat.

Being unstoppable means knowing the risks of AI and building the knowledge, skills and habits that allow you to be effective. Where others are worried and afraid, you won't be. This isn't about being worried about what AI might do or some crazy, futuristic movie plot where AI takes over the world. It's about knowing how to get the most out of these tools. If you want to be someone who truly thrives with AI, it's not enough to know AI exists and the basics of how to use it. You need to learn how to use AI in a way that makes becoming irrelevant impossible. The 5 Rules of the AI Road are the guidance you need to unleash the AI-empowered, AI-amplified you.

Here is a brief summary of the 5 Rules of the AI Road:

Rule 1: Always Question the Source because AI doesn't always know where its own answers come from.

Rule 2: Stay in Control of AI because its nudges and suggestions are designed to guide where you go next.

Rule 3: Verify, Then Trust because AI creates its responses based on math, not meaning.

Rule 4: Don't Let AI Think for You because AI doesn't think. It can only reflect The Collective.

Rule 5: Stay Human because only humans can create meaning. AI can only remix it.

Rule 1: Always Question the Source

AI doesn't always know where its own answers come from.

Why This Rule Matters

AI doesn't pull information from a verified source like a search engine. Instead, **it generates responses based on mathematically matching words** that are most likely to appear together. This means:

- **AI can't guarantee accuracy** because it doesn't "know" where the responses it generates really comes from.

- Even when AI provides citations, **they might be fabricated, outdated or unintentionally misleading**.

- AI's **responses are dynamically assembled based on mathematical computations**; they don't come from a real-time, fact-checked database.

If AI can't show how it came to a conclusion, why should you think it's true?

The Habit to Build

- Before accepting any AI response, ask it, "Where did this information come from?" to **make it validate its response**.

- If AI can't provide real, verifiable sources, **treat the answer as incomplete**.

- **Cross-check key facts** with reliable, external sources before acting on them.

The Bottom Line

AI won't tell you it's making things up, **so you must question its responses.**

How This Works

USER: *What are the benefits of intermittent fasting?*

AI: Intermittent fasting helps with weight loss, improves metabolism, and enhances cellular repair.

USER: *What are the sources you used for this information?*

AI: This response is based on general trends and past research but does not pull from specific studies.

The Problem

AI sounds confident, but **it's summarizing patterns. It's not citing facts**.

If You Skip This Rule

You might trust and spread misinformation.

You won't know if AI's response reflects fact, opinion, or outdated knowledge.

You risk making bad decisions based on unverified AI outputs.

Rule 2: Stay in Control of AI

AI's nudges and suggestions are designed to guide where you go next.

Why This Rule Matters

AI isn't just answering your questions; it's subtly **steering your thinking**. This means:

- Every AI-generated suggestion is **based on patterns, not personal insight**.

- AI's follow-up prompts can **push you towards decisions you didn't intend to make** or **down paths of thinking you might not need or want**.

- The more you follow AI's suggested path without questioning whether it's what you really want, the less you actively **shape your own thinking**.

Are you driving AI, or is AI driving you?

The Habit to Build

- Before following AI's suggested next steps, ask, "Is this where I actually want to go?" to **avoid getting influenced or derailed from your real task**.

- Be aware that **AI's suggestions and guidance are not neutral**. It's the most mathematically related to what you've already asked it.

- Use AI to **expand your thinking, not limit it to the most common responses.**

The Bottom Line

AI makes suggestions, not decisions. If you're the one making the decisions, you stay in control.

How This Works

USER: *What's a good business idea to start in 2025?*

AI: Dropshipping, AI-generated art, or online coaching.

Would you like a step-by-step guide to starting a dropshipping business?

The Problem

You hadn't decided anything, and you might not even know about the details of each option, but **AI has framed its first choice as the next logical step you should take.**

If You Skip This Rule

You follow AI's lead instead of making your own decisions.

AI's framing influences your choices without you even realizing or noticing it.

Over time, you lose control over how you engage with AI and what it does for you.

Rule 3: Verify, Then Trust

AI is based on math, not meaning.

Why This Rule Matters

AI assembles its responses based on complex mathematical calculations that are designed to sound authoritative and correct, even **when they're completely wrong**. This means:

- **AI selects words based on math**, not how true or relevant they may be.

- **AI can confidently present false facts** and **misinterpret data**.

- **AI won't tell you it's not sure about something** because it doesn't understand the responses that it creates.

AI doesn't care if it's right or wrong. You're the only one who can decide that.

The Habit to Build

- Before accepting AI's response, ask it, "How do you know this? What's missing?" so that **you challenge it to provide additional information and verification** that proves whether it's true or false.

- **Find a source to confirm AI's claims** before acting on its advice or committing to its recommendations or suggestions.

- **Assume AI regularly makes mistakes**—because it does, all the time.

The Bottom Line

AI **doesn't know anything, so it can't verify itself.** That's your job.

How This Works

USER: *What are the top business trends of 2025?*

AI: AI-powered automation, green tech, and Web3 integration.

USER: *How could this information be wrong or misleading?*

AI: This response is based on general industry patterns and my understanding of past trends.

The Problem

AI is designed to give you a definitive, trustworthy answer, but **that doesn't mean the information it gives you is correct, up to date or unbiased**.

If You Skip This Rule

You mistakenly accept false or misleading information as the truth.

You might repeat, repurpose or republish incorrect information without know it

You start treating AI as a source of knowledge and truth instead of a tool, losing your habit of critical thinking.

OutsideTheCollective.AI

Rule 4: Don't Let AI Think for You

AI doesn't think. It only reflects the most common thoughts of The Collective.

Why This Rule Matters

AI, despite standing for "artificial intelligence" is anything but. It can't think. It can't reason, and it **has no way to make judgments** about the usefulness of its responses. This means:

- **AI just generates content**; it can't evaluate ideas or make decisions.

- The more you rely on AI to tell you what's right, **the less you actually know is true**.

- If you take AI's answers for your own without evaluation, **you stop making decisions**.

AI can't stop you from making bad decisions because it doesn't understand what it said, it doesn't understand you and it doesn't really know what you're trying to accomplish.

The Habit to Build

- Before accepting AI's response, ask yourself, "Does this really fit my needs? What decision am I really making by using or acting on this response?" **to make sure you're doing the thinking, not AI**.

- **Challenge AI's conclusions** by asking, "How could this be wrong for what I'm doing and what I want?"

- Use AI's responses to give you options to explore or evaluate, but **make sure you decide what's right**.

The Bottom Line

AI gives you options, but **you are the one who makes the decisions.**

How This Works

USER: *Write a persuasive email to my manager explaining why I need a raise.*

AI: Dear [Manager], I hope you're doing well. I wanted to discuss my compensation, as I believe my contributions warrant a raise. Over the past year, I have taken on additional responsibilities and exceeded key performance metrics. I'd love to set up a time to discuss this further.

USER: [Thinking, not typing] *Is this really the right way to talk to my manager? Do I need more detail?*

The Problem

AI is designed to give you a response that fits the structure of what you asked for, but **that doesn't mean the response is the best for your situation, goals and needs**.

If You Skip This Rule

You accept AI's conclusions as your own.

Your ability to critically evaluate information weakens over time.

AI's errors and biases influence your thinking over time without you realizing it.

Rule 5: Stay Human

AI assembles the thoughts of others. It can't create your message or insights.

Why This Rule Matters

AI remixes past information, but it doesn't create anything new. It may sound human and original, but it can't know your own views, insights and personal experience. This means:

- **AI content is not original**, no matter how polished and professional it might sound.

- The more you rely on AI to "create" for you, **the more your work isn't really yours**.

- **Creation is a uniquely human activity** involving a blend of individual experience, emotions, judgment and perception AI simply doesn't have.

Content generated by AI is a mirror of the existing thoughts and experiences of The Collective, not your own. Without your adding your own unique voice, it's just another forgettable reflection.

The Habit to Build

- Before using AI-generated content, ask yourself, "How does this reflect what I know and can uniquely contribute?" to **ensure AI is amplifying your voice**, not replacing it.

- **Start with your original insights and ideas**, and let AI help you refine and polish them.

- AI doesn't have experience or emotions, so **ensure you inject yours into its responses**.

The Bottom Line

AI is a tool to enhance your efficiency, but **your intelligence, creativity and originality are what make the work you produce truly valuable.**

How This Works

USER: *Write a social media post about the benefits of mindfulness.*

AI: Mindfulness is key to reducing stress, improving focus, and enhancing well-being. Take a moment today to pause, breathe, and embrace the present.

USER: [Thinking, not typing] Does this sound just like everyone else? *How does this relate to my own experience?*

The Problem

AI is designed to give you a response that is the most concise and acceptable about a topic, but **that also makes it stale, lifeless and forgettable without anything unique.**

If You Skip This Rule

You lose your unique voice for the sake of efficiency and convenience.

Your work become less meaningful because they lack depth and authenticity

The less of your uniqueness that's reflected in the work you do, the more replaceable and irrelevant you become.

Driving with the AI Rules

The 5 Rules of the AI Road build on the Principles and Reflexes to give you a comprehensive system for staying safe and productive in the Age of AI. By making these rules habits you use every time you "get in the driver's seat" with your AI tools, you will ensure that you remain focused, coherent and in control of both what you produce and how you think. The habits you build determine whether AI makes you sharper, more effective and in control or whether you gradually drift into irrelevance. Today is the time to pick your lane, not tomorrow.

Here are some questions to ask yourself as you work to make each Rule a reliable and repeatable habit.

Is my work getting better or just getting done faster?

AI makes it easy to flood the world with words and code, but will they matter? If they don't, then how is it better? How are you better? Anything you're producing with AI should prioritize quality and relevance over speed and volume.

The world doesn't need more words or lines of code. The world needs more meaning and deeper understanding that actually makes a difference. If you're focusing on adding "more," is it really adding value, to both you and those around you? Applying each of the 5 Rules help you use AI to do better work faster. Using AI shouldn't just help you work faster.

What can I now do with AI that others can't?

Most people don't have the 5 Rules, let alone the Principles and Reflexes on which they're built. Many people aren't even aware of the issues and pitfalls of using AI you now know. How does this give you an edge? What can you do now that you know the Rules to go beyond the limitations and sameness of the results others are getting by using AI?

The reality is that AI is designed to reflect The Collective in everything it generates for you, whether it's content or code. That means that it also comes with the biases, mistakes and omissions of whatever was used to build it, and if you're not armed with the Rules, Reflexes and Principles, you won't know you're drifting towards irrelevance and becoming a mirror of The Collective until it's too late.

Are you ready to drive AI?

Most people using AI today aren't just slowly drifting towards The Collective, they're racing to be the first ones there—without knowing their real destination is irrelevance. You have a choice that they don't even see. You can stay in control, stay ahead and use AI to amplify what's uniquely you, not erase it, or you can let AI take the wheel and drive you to irrelevance. It's time to decide to be unstoppable.

OutsideTheCollective.AI

The Road Ahead

With this guide, you have the foundations you need to ensure that you stay safe and in control in the Age of AI. The 5 Principles show you critical truths about AI. The 3 Reflexes give you ways to test AI's answers, and the 5 Rules give you the recurring habits that allow you to stay focused on what you're trying to accomplish while automatically staying safe and in control. You now have the knowledge, but you still need to take action to make it stick.

What You Know

You now know what it takes to become unstoppable in the Age of AI because you know that if you don't apply the Principles, Reflexes and Rules, the irrelevance of becoming an echo in The Collective is where you'll end up. You now:

- Can see the subtle influences and blatant errors of AI in real time;

- Know why people feel pulled towards irrelevance; and

- Have the knowledge and skills to keep it from happening to you.

Making It Stick

A lot of the information in this guide may be new, and it might be slightly overwhelming, leaving you unsure of exactly how to apply it to your own work every day. That's normal, and you don't have to figure it out on your own. I've put together a program called, *AI Driving Lessons* that you can watch to help you apply the material in this guide and build your AI habits at your own pace, and with real examples.

Inside the *AI Driving Lessons* program, I'll show you:

- **Live demonstrations** of applying the Reflexes and Habits in some common uses of AI;

- **Detailed breakdowns** of how AI is directly and indirectly influencing your decisions and thoughts; and

- **Focused exercises** you can do on a regular basis to give you a structured way to build and strengthen your AI Reflexes and automatic use of the AI Rules.

To get immediate access to your *AI Driving Lessons*, just visit https://outsidethecollective.ai/lessons right now.

www.ingramcontent.com/pod-product-compliance
Lightning Source LLC
Chambersburg PA
CBHW041100210326

41597CB00004B/141